Car~~~

Cookbook

Introduction

Carrots are a bright, sweet spring vegetable that is delicious and good for you with many health benefits.

Carrots are very high in vitamins A, C and K, plus copper and iron. The biggest health benefits from carrots are from the large amounts of beta-carotene and fiber that they have.

Carrots have been shown to lower cholesterol and blood pressure. Carrots are great immune boosters due to the large amounts of vitamin C and other vitamins. Of course, many people know that carrots are good for your eyes. This is due to the lare amounts of vitamin A.

This cookbook contains a bevy of delicious mouth-watering carrot recipes for you to try. With all the great health benefits of carrots and the great taste, why not use these recipes to get chopping!

Celery and Carrot Soup

Ingredients:

2 tbsps. extra virgin olive oil
1 small onion, minced
1 small carrot, peeled and thinly sliced
1 celery rib, thinly sliced
1/2 tsp. dried tarragon
2 cups vegetable broth
1/2 cup dry white wine

Directions:

1. Heat the oil in a medium saucepan over medium-high heat.
2. Sauté onions until tender, approximately 5 minutes.
3. Slowly stir in carrots, celery, and tarragon, and continue cooking another 5 minutes, or until carrots are tender.
4. Stir in vegetable broth and wine, and bring to a boil.
5. Reduce to a simmer, and continue cooking 15 minutes longer. Serve hot.

Curried Carrot Soup

Ingredients:

2 tbsps. vegetable oil
1 onion, chopped
1 tbsp. curry powder
2 lbs. carrots, chopped
4 cups vegetable broth
2 cups water, or as needed

Directions:

1. Heat oil in a large pot over medium heat.
2. Sauté onion until tender and translucent.
3. Stir in the curry powder.
4. Add the chopped carrots, and stir until the carrots are coated.
5. Pour in the vegetable broth, and simmer until the carrots are soft, about 20 minutes.
6. Transfer the carrots and broth to a blender, and puree until smooth.
7. Pour back into the pot, and thin with water to your preferred consistency.

Herb Carrot Soup

Ingredients:

1 tbsp. butter
1 tbsp. all-purpose flour
1 cup half-and-half
1 1/2 cups vegetable broth
2 1/2 cups sliced carrots
1 tbsp. chopped fresh parsley
1 tbsp. chopped fresh basil
1 tsp. ground cayenne pepper
Salt to taste
Ground black pepper to taste

Directions:

1. Steam carrots until tender.
2. In a blender or food processor, combine cooked carrots and 3/4 cup broth.
3. Blend until smooth. Set aside.
4. In a medium saucepan, melt butter over medium heat.
5. Stir in flour, parsley, basil, and ground red pepper.
6. Add half-and-half cream all at once.
7. Cook and stir until slightly thickened and bubbly.
8. Stir in carrot mixture and remaining broth.
9. Season with salt and black pepper.
10. Thin with milk or water if needed.

Carrot and Cauliflower Curried Soup

Ingredients:

6 carrots, peeled and chopped
1/2 head cauliflower, chopped
1 1/2 tsps. olive oil
2 cloves garlic, chopped
1 tsp. salt
1 tsp. ground black pepper
3 cups vegetable broth, or more if needed
1 tbsp. curry powder
1 cup coconut milk
1/2 lime, juiced

Directions:

1. Preheat oven to 400 degrees F (200 degrees C).
2. Place carrots and cauliflower in a casserole dish; toss with olive oil, garlic, salt, and black pepper.
3. Roast carrot mixture in the preheated oven for 20 minutes; stir and roast until vegetables are tender and slightly charred, another 25 minutes.
4. Remove from oven and stir.
5. Bring vegetable broth to a boil in a large pot.
6. Stir in curry powder and add the roasted vegetables.
7. Cover and boil soup until vegetables are soft, 8 to 10 minutes.
8. Remove from heat.
9. Blend the soup with a potato masher or an immersion blender until smooth. Return pot to burner on medium heat.
10. Stir coconut milk and lime juice into soup.
11. Simmer until heated through, 5 to 10 minutes.

Carrot Coconut Lime Soup

Ingredients:

2 tbsps. olive oil
2 tsps. chile paste
1 tsp. cumin
1 tbsp. chopped fresh cilantro
1 tsp. grated fresh ginger
2 onions, chopped
2 cloves garlic, minced
2 large potatoes, peeled and chopped
6 large carrots, peeled and chopped
3 cups vegetable broth
7 cups coconut milk
1/4 cup lime juice
2 tbsps. chopped fresh cilantro

Directions:

1. Heat oil in a large Dutch oven over medium heat.
2. Stir and cook the chili paste, cumin, and
3. 1 tbsp. of cilantro until fragrant, about 1 minute.
4. Add the ginger, onion, and garlic; cook until the onions are soft and translucent, about 5 minutes.
5. Place the potatoes and carrots into the pot with the onion mixture and cook for an additional 5 minutes.
6. Pour the vegetable broth and coconut milk over the cooked vegetables.
7. Turn the heat to medium-high and bring to a boil, stirring occasionally.
8. Reduce the heat to medium-low and simmer for 30 to 45 minutes or until the potatoes and carrots are soft.
9. Remove the Dutch oven from the heat and stir in the lime juice.
10. Puree the soup in a blender or food processor until smooth.
11. Garnish with cilantro.

Sweet Potato and Carrot Soup

Ingredients:

2 tbsps. butter
1 onion, diced
1/2 tsp. ground cardamom
1/4 tsp. ground turmeric
1/4 tsp. ground ginger
1/4 tsp. red pepper flakes
1/4 tsp. ground cinnamon
1 pinch cayenne pepper
1 (14 oz.) can chicken broth
2 cups water
2 large sweet potatoes, peeled and diced
3 carrots, peeled and chopped
Salt and pepper to taste

Directions:

1. Melt the butter in a large saucepan over medium-high heat.
2. Stir in onions, and cook until golden brown, 5 to 7 minutes.
3. Season with cardamom, turmeric, ginger, pepper flakes, cinnamon, cayenne; cook until fragrant, about 1 minute.
4. Pour in chicken broth and water.
5. Add sweet potatoes and carrots.
6. Bring to a boil over high heat, then reduce heat to medium-low, cover, and simmer until the vegetables are tender, 25 to 30 minutes.
7. Remove from heat, and puree in batches until smooth.

Potato, Carrot, Lentil Soup

Ingredients:

1/4 cup butter
2 large sweet potatoes, peeled and chopped
3 large carrots, peeled and chopped
1 apple, peeled, cored and chopped
1 onion, chopped
1/2 cup red lentils
1/2 tsp. minced fresh ginger
1/2 tsp. ground black pepper
1 tsp. salt
1/2 tsp. ground cumin
1/2 tsp. chili powder
1/2 tsp. paprika
4 cups vegetable broth plain yogurt

Directions:

1. Melt the butter in a large, heavy bottomed pot over medium-high heat.
2. Place the chopped sweet potatoes, carrots, apple, and onion in the pot.
3. Stir and cook the apples and vegetables until the onions are translucent, about 10 minutes.
4. Stir the lentils, ginger, ground black pepper, salt, cumin, chili powder, paprika, and vegetable broth into the pot with the apple and vegetable mixture.
5. Bring the soup to a boil over high heat, then reduce the heat to medium-low, cover, and simmer until the lentils and vegetables are soft, about 30 minutes.
6. Working in batches, pour the soup into a blender, filling the pitcher no more than halfway full.
7. Hold down the lid of the blender with a folded kitchen towel, and carefully start the blender, using a few quick pulses to get the soup moving before leaving it on to puree.
8. Puree until smooth and pour into a clean pot.
9. Return the pureed soup to the cooking pot.
10. Bring back to a simmer over medium-high heat, about 10 minutes.
11. Add water as needed to thin the soup to your preferred consistency.
12. Serve with yogurt for garnish.

Carrot, Potato, and Cabbage Soup

Ingredients:

4 large carrots, thinly sliced
2 large potatoes, thinly sliced
1 large onion, thinly sliced
1/4 med. head green cabbage, thinly sliced
2 cloves garlic, smashed
6 cups chicken stock
1 tbsp. olive oil
1/4 tsp. dried thyme
1/4 tsp. dried basil
1 tsp. dried parsley
1 tsp. salt
Ground black pepper to taste

Directions:

1. Combine the carrots, potatoes, onion, cabbage, garlic, chicken stock, olive oil, thyme, basil, parsley, salt, and pepper in a stock pot over medium-high heat.
2. Bring to a simmer and cook until the carrots are tender, about 20 minutes.
3. Transfer to a blender in small batches and blend until smooth.

Ginger Carrot Soup

Ingredients:

1 tbsp. olive oil
2 large yellow onions, chopped
1 lb. carrots, cut in chunks
2 cups chicken broth
2 tbsps. crystallized ginger, minced
1 tsp. cinnamon
1 1/2 cups orange juice
1/2 cup half-and-half
Chives for garnish

Directions:

1. In a large pot, sauté onions in olive oil until soft.
2. Add carrots, broth, ginger and cinnamon. Simmer until carrots are thoroughly cooked, 30-40 minutes.
3. Transfer to a blender or food processor and process until smooth.
4. Stir in juice and half-and-half.
5. Garnish with chives.

Cream Of Carrot Soup

Ingredients:

1/4 cup butter, cubed
2 1/2 cups sliced carrots
1 large potato, peeled and cubed
1 cup chopped onion
1 stalk celery, chopped
3 cups chicken broth
1 tsp. ground ginger
1/2 cup heavy whipping cream
1 tsp. curry powder
1/2 tsp. salt
1/8 tsp. ground black pepper

Directions:

1. Heat butter in a Dutch oven over medium heat.
2. Add carrots, potato, onion, celery, chicken broth, and ginger.
3. Cover and cook, stirring occasionally, until vegetables are tender, about 30 minutes. Uncover and cool for 15 minutes.
4. Transfer soup in batches to a food processor.
5. Blend until smooth. Return soup to the Dutch oven.
6. Stir in cream.
7. Add curry powder, salt, and black pepper; cook over low heat until heated through, about 10 minutes.

Carrot Slaw

Ingredients:

5 carrots, coarsely grated
1/4 cup sunflower seeds
1/4 cup oil and vinegar salad

Directions:

1. Toss carrots and sunflower seeds in a bowl with the salad dressing.
2. Serve and enjoy!

Russian Carrot Salad

Ingredients:

6 large carrots, shredded
3 cloves garlic, minced
1/4 cup finely chopped walnuts
1/4 cup light mayonnaise

Directions:

1. Stir together the carrots, garlic, walnuts, and mayonnaise until evenly blended.
2. Serve and enjoy!

Russian Carrot Salad (Korean-Style)

Ingredients:

1 lb. carrots, peeled and julienned
3 cloves garlic, minced
1/4 cup vinegar
1 tbsp. white sugar
2 1/2 tsps. salt
1/3 cup vegetable oil
1/2 onion, minced
1 tsp. ground coriander
1/2 tsp. cayenne pepper

Directions:

1. Place carrots in a large bowl.
2. Sprinkle garlic over carrots.
3. Mix vinegar, sugar, and salt together in a small bowl.
4. Heat oil in a skillet over medium heat.
5. Cook and stir onion in hot oil until soft and translucent, 5 to 7 minutes.
6. Stir coriander and cayenne pepper into the onion; add to carrot mixture and toss.
7. Pour vinegar dressing over carrot mixture; toss to coat.
8. Transfer carrot salad to a dish with a tight-fitting lid, cover, and refrigerate 4 to 24 hours, tossing salad several times while it marinates.

Carrot and Peanut Salad

Ingredients:

2 cups grated carrots
1/2 cup chopped salted peanuts
3 tbsps. lemon juice
1/2 tsp. salt
1 tsp. white sugar
1 green chile pepper, seeded and diced
2 tbsps. fresh cilantro, chopped

Directions:

1. In a medium serving bowl, toss together the carrots and peanuts.
2. In a separate bowl, whisk together the lemon juice, salt, sugar, chile pepper and cilantro.
3. Pour over the carrots and stir gently to coat. Serve immediately.

Indian Carrot Salad

Ingredients:

2 cups grated carrots
1/2 cup chopped cilantro
1 tbsp. crushed peanuts
2 tsps. lemon juice
1 tsp. white sugar
1/2 tsp. salt
2 sprigs cilantro, for garnish

Directions:

1. Toss carrots, chopped cilantro, and crushed peanuts together in a large bowl.
2. Stir lemon juice, sugar, and salt into carrot mixture.
3. Set aside long enough to allow the sugar to dissolve, about 10 minutes.
4. Garnish with cilantro and serve.

Citrus Carrot Salad

Ingredients:

1 cup shredded carrots
1/4 cup raisins
1 tsp. lemon juice
1 tsp. lime juice
1 tsp. white sugar
1 tbsp. miniature marshmallows

Directions:

1. Mix carrots, raisins, lemon juice, lime juice, and sugar together using a fork in a microwave-safe bowl; cover bowl.
2. Heat in the microwave on low for 30 seconds. Transfer salad to a glass bowl; sprinkle marshmallows over salad.

Rainbow Carrot Salad

Ingredients:

1 bunch rainbow carrots
2 tbsps. olive oil
2 tbsps. rice wine vinegar
1 tsp. fresh lemon juice
1/4 tsp. ground cumin
Salt and freshly ground black pepper to taste
2 green onions, sliced

Directions:

1. Using short strokes with a vegetable peeler, shave carrots into thin shavings about 2 inches long.
2. Whisk olive oil, rice wine vinegar, lemon juice, and cumin together in a bowl; pour over carrots and toss gently with a rubber spatula.
3. Season carrots with salt and pepper; sprinkle with green onions.

Ginger Carrot Salad

Ingredients:

1 pound carrots, cut diagonally into thin slices
2 tbsps. cider vinegar
1 tbsp. olive oil
2 tbsps. Splenda
1 clove garlic, grated
1/4 tsp. ground cumin
1/4 tsp. cinnamon
1 tsp. grated fresh ginger
1/8 tsp. seasoned salt
1 dash cayenne pepper
1/2 cup raisins

Directions:

1. Bring a large pot of water to boil.
2. Add carrots, and continue to boil until just tender, about 2 minutes. Rinse with cold water, drain well, and set aside.
3. In a large bowl, whisk together vinegar, olive oil, Splenda, and garlic.
4. Season with cumin, cinnamon, ginger, salt, and cayenne pepper.
5. Stir in carrots and raisins, and toss with dressing.
6. Cover, and refrigerate at least 4 hours.

Carrot and Raisin Salad

Ingredients:

2 cups shredded carrots
1/2 cup diced celery
1/2 cup raisins
1/3 cup mayonnaise
1 tbsp. distilled white vinegar

Directions:

1. In a mixing bowl, combine the carrots, celery, raisins, mayonnaise and vinegar.
2. Mix together and refrigerate until chilled.

Tropical Carrot Raisin Salad

Ingredients:

1 cup raisins
1 lb. carrots, shredded
1/4 cup crushed pineapple in juice
3 tbsps. shredded coconut
1/4 tsp. salt
6 oz. pina colada yogurt
1/4 cup mayonnaise

Directions:

1. Soak raisins in a bowl of water until softened, about 20 minutes.
2. Drain.
3. Combine carrots, raisins, pineapple, coconut, and salt in a bowl.
4. Mix yogurt and mayonnaise in another bowl.
5. Stir into carrot mixture.
6. Cover and refrigerate until chilled.

Drunken Raison Carrot Salad

Ingredients:

1/3 cup golden raisins
1/2 cup Chardonnay white wine
2 cups shredded carrots
1/4 cup mayonnaise

Directions:

1. Soak raisins in Chardonnay white wine in a bowl until plump, about 1 hour.
2. Drain and reserve any remaining liquid from the plumped raisins.
3. Mix carrots, mayonnaise, and chives together in a large bowl.
4. Fold plumped raisins into carrot mixture.
5. Mix reserved soaking liquid into the salad a tbsp. at a time until desired texture is achieved.

Zucchini and Carrot Coleslaw

Ingredients:

2 cups shredded zucchini
1 cup shredded carrot
1/4 cup salad dressing (such as Miracle Whip)
1 tsp. sugar

Directions:

1. Salt and ground black pepper to taste
2. Place zucchini in a colander and let drain thoroughly, about 30 minutes.
3. Toss with carrot in a large salad bowl.
4. Stir in creamy salad dressing and sugar.
5. Chill the coleslaw for 1 hour to blend flavors, stir again, and season with salt and black pepper.

Carrot and Radish Salad

Ingredients:

1 tbsp. Meyer lemon-infused olive oil
1 tsp. peach-infused balsamic vinegar
1 pinch garlic powder
Salt and ground black pepper to taste
1 large carrot
1/3 daikon radish
1 tbsp. slivered almonds
1 tbsp. shredded coconut
1 tsp. snipped fresh chives

Directions:

1. Whisk lemon-infused olive oil, peach-infused vinegar, garlic powder, salt, and pepper together in a bowl to make vinaigrette.
2. Attach carrot to a spiralizer and cut into ribbons.
3. Toss with vinaigrette in the bowl. Let stand until slightly softened, about 10 minutes.
4. Attach radish to the spiralizer and cut into ribbons.
5. Toss with carrot mixture in the bowl. Garnish with almonds, coconut, and chives.

Carrot Ambrosia Salad

Ingredients:

1/2 cup yogurt
1/2 cup pineapple tidbits in pineapple juice, undrained
1/2 cup raisins
1/2 cup coconut
2 tbsps. honey, or to taste 4 cups spiral-sliced carrots

Directions:

1. Stir yogurt, pineapple, raisins, coconut, and honey together in a bowl; add carrots.
2. Stir until ingredients are thoroughly combined. Refrigerate until chilled, about 30 minutes.
3. Stir again before serving.

Carrot Cucumber Salad

Ingredients:

1/4 cup seasoned rice vinegar
1 tsp. white sugar
1/2 tsp. vegetable oil
1/4 tsp. grated peeled ginger
1/4 tsp. salt
1 cup sliced carrot
2 tbsps. sliced green onion
2 tbsps. minced red bell pepper
1/2 cucumber - halved lengthwise, seeded, and sliced

Directions:

1. Whisk rice vinegar, sugar, vegetable oil, ginger, and salt together in a bowl until sugar and salt are dissolved into a smooth dressing.
2. Toss carrot, green onion, bell pepper, and cucumber in the dressing to evenly coat.
3. Cover bowl with plastic wrap and refrigerate until chilled, about 30 minutes.

Mexican Carrot and Cucumber Salad

Ingredients:

1 cucumber, sliced
1 (8 oz.) pkg. baby carrots
1 lime, juiced
1 tsp. chili powder
1/4 tsp. salt
1 pinch cayenne pepper

Directions:

1. Combine the cucumber, baby carrots, lime juice, chili powder, salt, and cayenne pepper in a bowl.
2. Toss to combine.

Beet and Carrot Lentil Salad

Ingredients:

1 cup water, or as needed 3 small beets, greens removed 3 cups water
1 cup French lentils
1/2 tsp. salt 5 vine-ripened tomatoes, chopped
4 carrots, shredded
1/2 bunch fresh cilantro, finely chopped 5 green onions, chopped
3 lemons, zested and juiced

Directions:

1. Pour enough water into a baking dish to cover bottom with about 1/2 inch of water; add beets.
2. Bake in the preheated oven until beets are tender when poked with a fork, about 45 minutes. Transfer beets to bowl of cold water until cool enough to handle.
3. Bring 3 cups water to a boil in saucepan; add lentils and salt.
4. Reduce heat and simmer until lentils are tender, about 20 minutes.
5. Drain.
6. Remove beets from water, pat dry, and slice ends and outer skin off each beet. Roughly chop beets and grate in the food processor.
7. Mix beets, lentils, tomatoes, carrots, cilantro, green onions, lemon zest, and lemon juice together in a bowl; season with salt.

Sweet And Sour Carrots

Ingredients:

2 cups carrots, sliced
1/2 cup celery, sliced
1 can (8 oz.) pineapple tidbits, drained, juice reserved
1 tbsp. vinegar
2 tsps. cornstarch
1 tsp. light soy sauce
1/8 tsp. salt
2 tbsps. stick butter
1/4 cup sliced green onions
1/4 cup Equal (6 packets)

Directions:

1. Cook carrots and celery in medium saucepan in small amount of water about 8 minutes or until tender.
2. Drain; set aside.
3. Add enough water to reserved pineapple juice to make 1/2 cup liquid.
4. Stir in vinegar, cornstarch, soy sauce and salt.
5. Cook in medium saucepan until liquid thickens, stirring frequently.
6. Add butter, drained pineapple, and onions. Continue stirring until all ingredients are heated.
7. Add drained carrots and celery.
8. Cook about 2 minutes.
9. Stir in Equal.

Glazed Carrots

Ingredients:

6 carrots, peeled, cooked whole
1/4 tsp. salt
1 tbsp. cornstarch
1/4 cup sugar
1/2 cup water
2 tbsps. butter
1/4 cup vinegar
2 cloves sticks (optional)

Directions:

1. In a covered saucepan, simmer carrots in barely enough lightly salted water to cover until tender but firm.
2. Remove carrots from pot; drain and set aside.
3. In the same saucepan, combine salt, sugar, cornstarch, cloves and cold water.
4. Stir until cornstarch has dissolved.
5. Bring to a boil and reduce heat to a simmer; cook until clear and slightly thickened.
6. Add butter and vinegar.
7. Remove cloves.
8. Pour sauce over carrots and serve.

Honey Glazed Carrots

Ingredients:

3 tbsp. honey
2 tbsp. Dijon mustard
1 tbsp. vegetable oil
5 carrots, pealed and copped to bite sized pieces
2 tbsp. green onions, sliced

Directions:

1. Combine honey, mustard and oil in a large skillet.
2. Bring to a boil over medium-high heat.
3. Boil 1 to 2 minutes or until thickened, stirring constantly.
4. Add carrots and cook 5 minutes or until glazed; gently stir occasionally.
5. Season to taste with salt and black pepper and top with green onions.

Maple Cinnamon Glazed Carrots

Ingredients:

1/4 cup maple syrup
1 tbsp. cider vinegar
1/4 tsp. cinnamon
1 tbsp. vegetable oil
5 carrots, pealed and copped to bite sized pieces
2 tbsp. green onions, sliced

Directions:

1. Combine maple syrup, vinegar and oil in a large skillet.
2. Bring to a boil over medium-high heat.
3. Boil 1 to 2 minutes or until thickened, stirring constantly.
4. Add carrots and cook 5 minutes or until glazed; gently stir occasionally.
5. Season to taste with salt and black pepper and top with green onions.

Lemon Pepper Glazed Carrots

Ingredients:

1 tbsp. fresh lemon juice
1/8 tsp. ground black pepper
1 tbsp. vegetable oil
5 carrots, pealed and copped to bite sized pieces
2 tbsp. green onions, sliced

Directions:

1. Combine lemon juice, pepper and oil in a large skillet.
2. Bring to a boil over medium-high heat.
3. Boil 1 to 2 minutes or until thickened, stirring constantly.
4. Add carrots and cook 5 minutes or until glazed; gently stir occasionally.
5. Season to taste with salt and black pepper and top with green onions.

Hawaiian Style Glazed Carrots

Ingredients:

1 can (8 oz.) crushed pineapple
1 tbsp. soy sauce
1 tbsp. vegetable oil
5 carrots, pealed and copped to bite sized pieces
2 tbsp. green onions, sliced

Directions:

1. Combine pineapple, soy sauce and oil in a large skillet.
2. Bring to a boil over medium-high heat.
3. Boil 1 to 2 minutes or until thickened, stirring constantly.
4. Add carrots and cook 5 minutes or until glazed; gently stir occasionally.
5. Season to taste with salt and black pepper and top with green onions.

Orange Spiced Glazed Carrots

Ingredients:

1/4 cup orange juice,
2 tbsp. sugar and
1/8 tsp. cayenne pepper
1 tbsp. vegetable oil
5 carrots, pealed and copped to bite sized pieces
2 tbsp. green onions, sliced

Directions:

1. Combine orange juice, sugar, cayenne pepper and oil in a large skillet.
2. Bring to a boil over medium-high heat.
3. Boil 1 to 2 minutes or until thickened, stirring constantly.
4. Add carrots and cook 5 minutes or until glazed; gently stir occasionally.
5. Season to taste with salt and black pepper and top with green onions.

Orange Juice Carrots

Ingredients:

5-6 carrots
1/2 cup orange juice
1 3/4 cups cold water
1/2 tsp. salt
2 tbsps. sugar
3 tbsps. butter
1 tbsp. flour
1/2 cup additional boiling water

Directions:

1. Wash, peel and slice the carrots.
2. Place in a saucepan and add the orange juice, salt, sugar and cold water.
3. Bring to a boil, skim carefully, reduce heat, cover and simmer over very low heat until fork tender, about 1 1/4 hours.
4. Watch carefully and shake the pan occasionally to prevent sticking.
5. When tender, add 1/2 cup additional boiling water.
6. Stir in 3 tbsps. butter mixed with 1 tbsp. flour to thicken (cream until smooth before adding).
7. Cook for several minutes and serve.

Carrot Cake Protein Smoothie

Ingredients:

5 oz. carrots, chopped
1 banana
1/2 tsp. cinnamon
2 dates, pitted
3 tbsp. walnuts
1 tbsp. pea protein
1 cup vanilla almond milk
1 cup ice

Directions:

1. Add all ingredients to a blender or food processor.
2. Blend until smooth.
3. Serve and enjoy!

Carrot Coconut Smoothie

Ingredients:

6 oz. carrots - chopped
4 oz. pineapple
1 orange - peeled
2 tbsp. coconut flakes
1 tsp. camu camu
1 cup water1 cup ice

Directions:

1. Add all ingredients to a blender or food processor.
2. Blend until smooth.
3. Serve and enjoy!

Creamy Orange Carrot Smoothie

Ingredients:

4 oz. carrots, scrubbed and chopped
2 clementines, peeled
3 tbsp. cashews
2 tbsp. goji berries
1 cup rice milk
1 cup ice

Directions:

1. Add all ingredients to a blender or food processor.
2. Blend until smooth.
3. Serve and enjoy!

Carrot Coconut Lime Smoothie

Ingredients:

1.5 oz. kale
3 medium carrots
1 apple
1/2 lime, juiced
1 tbsp. shredded coconut
1 1/2 cup water
1 cup ice

Directions:

1. Add all ingredients to a blender or food processor.
2. Blend until smooth.
3. Serve and enjoy!

Carrot Goji Berries Smoothie

Ingredients:

1 1/2 cup carrots, chopped
2 oranges, peeled
2 tbsp. sunflower seeds
2 tbsp. goji berries
1/2 cup water
1 cup ice

Directions:

1. Add all ingredients to a blender or food processor.
2. Blend until smooth.
3. Serve and enjoy!

Candied Carrot Tops Smoothie

Ingredients:

1 handful carrot greens
1 carrot, chopped
1 cup grapes
1/2 tsp. camu camu powder
1 piece candied ginger
1 cup water
1 cup ice

Directions:

1. Add all ingredients to a blender or food processor.
2. Blend until smooth.
3. Serve and enjoy!

Ginger Lemonades Smoothie

Ingredients:

1 cup carrots, chopped
1 apple, chopped
1/2 lemon, juiced
1/2 inch ginger
1 tbsp. pumpkin seeds
1 cup water
1 cup ice

Directions:

1. Add all ingredients to a blender or food processor.
2. Blend until smooth.
3. Serve and enjoy!

Carrot Souffle

Ingredients:

1 lb. carrots, coarsely chopped
1/2 cup margarine
1 tsp. vanilla extract
3 eggs
3 tbsps. all-purpose flour
1 tsp. baking powder
1/2 tsp. salt
3/4 cup white sugar

Directions:

1. Preheat oven to 350 degrees F (175 degrees C).
2. Lightly grease a 2 quart casserole dish.
3. Bring a large pot of salted water to a boil.
4. Add carrots and cook until tender, 15 to 20 minutes.
5. Drain and mash.
6. Stir in margarine, vanilla extract and eggs; mix well.
7. Sift together flour, baking powder, salt and sugar.
8. Stir into carrot mixture and blend until smooth.
9. Transfer to prepared casserole dish.
10. Bake for 45 minutes.

Carrot Patties

Ingredients:

1 lb. carrots, grated
1 clove garlic, minced
4 eggs
1/4 cup all-purpose flour
1/4 cup bread crumbs or matzo meal
1/2 tsp. salt
1 pinch ground black pepper
2 tbsps. vegetable oil

Directions:

1. In a medium size mixing bowl, combine the grated carrots, garlic, eggs, flour, bread crumbs, salt and black pepper; mix well.
2. Heat oil in a frying pan over medium-high heat.
3. Make the mixture into patties, and fry until golden brown on each side.

Carrot Casserole with Cheese

Ingredients:

8 cups sliced carrots
1 large onion, diced
1 tbsp. butter
1/4 cup heavy cream
1/2 tsp. salt
1/2 tsp. ground black pepper
1 1/2 cups processed cheese food
1/2 cup fine dry bread crumbs

Directions:

1. Preheat oven to 350 degrees F (175 degrees C).
2. Bring a large pot of salted water to a boil.
3. Add carrots and cook until tender but still firm, about 15 minutes.
4. Drain and place in a 2 quart casserole dish.
5. Stir in onion, butter, cream, salt, pepper and cheese; mix well.
6. Sprinkle bread crumbs over the top and bake for 50 minutes.

Carrot Turnip Casserole

Ingredients:

1 (8 oz.) pkg. instant stuffing mix
1 turnip, chopped
2 lbs. carrots, chopped
2 tbsps. butter, melted
2 tbsps. brown sugar
1 (8 oz.) pkg. processed cheese, shredded
2 tbsps. milk

Directions:

1. Preheat oven to 350 degrees F (175 degrees C).
2. Lightly grease a medium casserole dish.
3. Prepare the stuffing according to package directions.
4. Place turnip and carrots in a pot with enough water to cover, and bring to a boil.
5. Cook until tender.
6. Drain, and mash.
7. Mix in butter and brown sugar until melted.
8. Place processed cheese food in a microwave-safe bowl, and melt in the microwave.
9. Stir in milk, and mix into the mashed vegetables. Transfer to the prepared casserole dish. Top with the stuffing.
10. Bake 20 minutes in the preheated oven, until golden brown.

Carrot Zucchini Casserole

Ingredients:

1 lb. carrots, sliced
3 zucchinis, slice
1/2 cup mayonnaise
2 tbsps. grated onion
3/4 tsp. prepared horseradish
1/2 tsp. salt
1/2 tsp. ground black pepper
1/2 cup Italian bread crumbs
1/4 cup butter, melted

Directions:

1. Preheat the oven to 375 degrees F (190 degrees C).
2. Lightly grease a 9x13-inch baking dish.
3. Place carrots into a pot and cover with salted water; bring to a boil.
4. Reduce heat to medium-low and simmer until just tender, about 15 minutes. Strain carrots out of the water with a slotted spoon.
5. Add zucchini slices to the pot and simmer until tender, 2 to 3 minutes.
6. Drain, reserving about 1/4 cup cooking liquid.
7. Stir reserved cooking liquid into mayonnaise, onion, horseradish, salt, and black pepper in a large bowl.
8. Mix cooked vegetables into mayonnaise mixture until well blended; pour mixture into prepare baking dish.
9. Mix bread crumbs and melted butter in a small bowl; sprinkle over vegetables.
10. Bake in preheated oven until bread crumbs are lightly browned, about 15 minutes.

Carrot Cake

Ingredients:

6 cups grated carrots
1 cup brown sugar
1 cup raisins
4 eggs
1 1/2 cups white sugar
1 cup vegetable oil
2 tsps. vanilla extract
1 cup crushed pineapple, drained
3 cups all-purpose flour
1 1/2 tsps. baking soda
1 tsp. salt 4 tsps. ground cinnamon
1 cup chopped walnuts

Directions:

1. In a medium bowl, combine grated carrots and brown sugar. Set aside for 60 minutes, then stir in raisins.
2. Preheat oven to 350 degrees F (175 degrees C).
3. Grease and flour two 10 inch cake pans.
4. In a large bowl, beat eggs until light.
5. Gradually beat in the white sugar, oil and vanilla.
6. Stir in the pineapple.
7. Combine the flour, baking soda, salt and cinnamon, stir into the wet mixture until absorbed. Finally stir in the carrot mixture and the walnuts.
8. Pour evenly into the prepared pans.
9. Bake for 45 to 50 minutes in the preheated oven, until cake tests done with a toothpick.
10. Cool for 10 minutes before removing from pan.
11. When completely cooled, frost with cream cheese frosting.

Swiss Carrot Cake

Ingredients:

5 egg yolks
1 1/4 cups white sugar
1 1/2 cups chopped almonds
2 cups grated carrots
1 lemon, zested and juiced
2/3 cup all-purpose flour
1 1/2 tsps. baking powder
5 egg whites
1 pinch salt
1 lemon, juiced
1 cup confectioners' sugar, or as needed

Directions:

1. Preheat the oven to 350 degrees F (175 degrees C).
2. Grease and flour a 9 inch square baking dish or 9 inch Bundt pan.
3. In a large bowl, whip egg yolks and sugar with an electric mixer until light and fl
4. ffy.
5. Stir in the almonds, carrots,1 lemon's juice and zest, flour and baking powder.
6. In a separate bowl with a clean beater, whip egg whites with a pinch of salt until they can hold a peak.
7. Fold egg whites into the carrot batter.
8. Pour into the prepared cake pan.
9. Bake for 50 minutes, or until a small knife inserted into the center comes out clean.
10. For icing, mix the remaining lemon's juice with confectioners' sugar until it can be drizzled easily from a spoon.
11. Pour over the cake while warm or cooled.
12. If making in a Bundt pan, remove from the pan before glazing.

Carrot Rice

Ingredients:

1 cup basmati rice
2 cups water
1/4 cup roasted peanuts
1 tbsp. margarine
1 onion, sliced
1 tsp. minced fresh ginger root
3/4 cup grated carrots
Salt to taste
Cayenne pepper to taste
Chopped fresh cilantro

Directions:

1. Combine rice and water in a medium saucepan.
2. Bring to a boil over high heat.
3. Reduce heat to low, cover with lid, and allow to steam until tender, about 20 minutes.
4. While rice is cooking, grind peanuts in a blender and set aside.
5. Heat the margarine in a skillet over medium heat.
6. Stir in the onion; cook and stir until the onion has softened and turned golden brown about 10 minutes.
7. Stir in ginger, carrots, and salt to taste.
8. Reduce heat to low and cover to steam 5 minutes.
9. Stir in cayenne pepper and peanuts.
10. When rice is done, add it to skillet and stir gently to combine with other ingredients.
11. Garnish with chopped cilantro.

Carrot Chips

Ingredients:

4 carrots, washed
2 tsps. extra-virgin olive oil
1/4 tsp. salt

Directions:

1. Preheat oven to 350 degrees F (175 degrees C).
2. Put one rack on the highest level in the oven and another on the bottom.
3. Peel carrots into thin strips using a vegetable peeler; put into a large bowl. Drizzle olive oil over the carrot strips and toss to coat.
4. Season with salt; toss again.
5. Spread carrots onto 2 baking sheets in a single layer, preventing overlap.
6. Put one baking sheet on the top rack and the other on the bottom.
7. Bake carrots in preheated oven for 6 minutes, switch racks, and continue baking until the carrots are crisp, about 6 minutes more.
8. Cool chips until cool enough to handle before serving.

Balsamic Glazed Carrots

Ingredients:

3 cups baby carrots
1 tbsp. olive oil
1 1/2 tbsps. balsamic vinegar
1 tbsp. brown sugar

Directions:

1. Heat oil in a skillet over medium-high heat.
2. Sauté carrots in oil for about 10 minutes, or until tender.
3. Stir in balsamic vinegar and brown sugar, mix to coat and serve.

Maple Glazed Carrots

Ingredients:

1 1/2 lbs. baby carrots
1/4 cup butter
1/3 cup maple syrup
Salt and ground black pepper to taste

Directions:

1. Place carrots into a pot and cover with salted water; bring to a boil.
2. Reduce heat to medium-low and simmer until tender, 15 to 20 minutes.
3. Drain and transfer carrots to a serving bowl.
4. Melt butter in a saucepan over medium-low heat.
5. Stir maple syrup into melted butter and cook until warmed, 1 to 2 more minutes.
6. Pour butter-maple syrup over carrots and toss to coat.
7. Season with salt and pepper.

Apricot Glazed Carrots

Ingredients:

2 lbs. carrots, peeled and sliced
3 tbsps. butter, melted
1/3 cup apricot preserves
1/4 tsp. ground nutmeg
1/4 tsp. salt
1 tsp. orange zest
2 tsps. fresh lemon juice chopped
Fresh parsley for garnish

Directions:

1. Add carrots to a pot of lightly salted water, and bring to a low boil
2. Simmer until carrots are tender.
3. Drain.
4. Put melted butter in a bowl, and stir in apricot preserves.
5. Stir in nutmeg, salt, orange zest, and lemon juice.
6. Add carrots, and stir well to coat.
7. Sprinkle with chopped parsley.

Orange Glazed Carrots

Ingredients:

1 lb. baby carrots
1/4 cup orange juice
3 tbsps. brown sugar
2 tbsps. butter
1 pinch salt

Directions:

1. Place carrots in a shallow saucepan, and cover with water. Boil until tender.
2. Drain, and return carrots to pan.
3. Pour orange juice over carrots, and mix well.
4. Simmer over medium heat for about 5 minutes.
5. Stir in brown sugar, butter, and salt.
6. Heat until butter and sugar melt.

Napa Roasted Vegetables

Ingredients:

2 cups carrots, cut into large pieces
2 cups butternut squash, cut into large pieces
2 cups sweet potatoes, cut into large pieces
2 cups red sweet potatoes, cut into thick pieces
4 cups Yukon Gold potatoes, cut into thick pieces
2 cups red onion, cut into wedges
1/2 cup olive oil
1 tsp. Sea Salt, divided
16 2 in. sprigs fresh thyme
1 tsp. crushed red pepper flakes
2 Granny Smith peeled, cut into large pieces
8 sprigs flat-leaf parsley, chopped

Directions:

1. Preheat oven to 400 degrees F (200 degrees C).
2. Place carrots, butternut squash, white and red sweet potatoes, and potatoes in separate containers.
3. Add water to cover; let soak for several minutes.
4. Drain.
5. Pour olive oil into large mixing bowl; add all the vegetables (not the apples) and toss to coat.
6. Stir in 3/4 tsp. Sea Salt, thyme and red pepper flakes.
7. Spread vegetables evenly on a 12x18-inch rimmed sheet pan.
8. Bake 30 minutes.
9. Stir vegetables and add the apple pieces.
10. Continue to bake for 30 minutes; stir again.
11. Bake until vegetables and apples are brown and tender, about 20 more minutes.
12. Transfer to serving dish; garnish with torn flat leaf parsley and remaining sea salt.

Carrots with Cognac

Ingredients:

3 cups baby carrots
1 tbsp. walnut oil
1/4 cup brandy
2 tsps. honey
1 tsp. ground cinnamon

Directions:

1. Preheat oven to 400 degrees F (200 degrees C).
2. Tear a large sheet of aluminum foil.
3. Place carrots on foil and sprinkle with walnut oil, cognac, honey, and cinnamon.
4. Wrap up tightly and roast for 25 to 35 minutes until carrots are tender, yet crisp.

Roasted Grapes and Carrots

Ingredients:

2 lbs. red seedless grapes
1 (16 oz.) package peeled, baby carrots
1 med. red onion, cut into wedges
2 tbsps. olive oil
1 tsp. ground cumin

Directions:

1. Preheat oven to 375 degrees F (190 degrees C).
2. Line a baking sheet with aluminum foil.
3. Toss together the grapes, carrots, and red onion in olive oil to coat.
4. Sprinkle with cumin and toss to evenly distribute.
5. Spread mixture on baking sheet.
6. Roast until carrots have begun to soften, about 15 to 20 minutes.

Roasted Parmesan-Garlic Carrots

Ingredients:

1 lb. carrots, peeled
1 tbsp. olive oil
1/2 tsp. garlic salt
1/4 cup grated Parmesan cheese

Directions:

1. Preheat oven to 375 degrees F (190 degrees C).
2. Line a baking sheet with aluminum foil.
3. Stir olive oil and garlic salt together in a small bowl; pour into a large re-sealable plastic bag.
4. Add carrots to the plastic bag, seal, and shake to coat carrots completely in oil mixture.
5. Arrange coated carrots onto the prepared baking sheet.
6. Roast carrots in preheated oven until crisp-tender, about 45 minutes.
7. Sprinkle 1/4 cup Parmesan cheese over carrots and continue roasting until cheese is lightly browned, 5 to 10 minutes.
8. Garnish with additional Parmesan cheese to serve.

Moroccan Carrots

Ingredients:

4 large carrots, peeled and grated
1 (16 oz.) can garbanzo beans, drained and rinsed
1/2 cup raisins
2 tbsps. olive oil
1 tbsp. lemon juice
1/2 tsp. cumin
1/2 tsp. chili powder
Salt and ground pepper to taste
1/4 cup crumbled feta cheese

Directions:

1. Combine carrots, garbanzo beans, and raisins together in a bowl.
2. Whisk olive oil, lemon juice, cumin, chili powder, salt, and ground black pepper together; stir into carrot mixture.
3. Marinate carrot mixture for 2 hours.
4. Serve with crumbled feta cheese.

Carrot Raisin Muffins

Ingredients:

2 cups whole wheat flour
1/2 cup all-purpose flour
1/8 tsp. salt
2 tsps. baking powder
1/4 tsp. ground nutmeg
1/4 tsp. ground cloves
1/4 tsp. ground cinnamon
2 eggs
1 cup buttermilk
1/4 cup vegetable oil
2 tbsps. applesauce
1/2 cup honey
1 1/2 cups shredded carrots
2/3 cup raisins

Directions:

1. Preheat oven to 400 degrees F (200 degrees C).
2. Grease 12 muffin cups or line with paper muffin liners.
3. Stir together whole wheat flour, all-purpose flour, salt, baking powder, nutmeg, cloves and cinnamon.
4. In a separate bowl, stir together eggs, buttermilk, oil, applesauce and honey.
5. Stir egg mixture into flour just until combined.
6. Fold in carrots and raisins.
7. Spoon batter into prepared muffin cups.
8. Bake in preheat oven for 18 minutes, or until a toothpick inserted into the center of a muffin comes out clean.

Carrot Spice Muffins

Ingredients:

1 1/2 cups all-purpose flour
1 1/2 cups wheat bran
1/4 cup wheat germ
1/2 cup brown sugar
1/2 tsp. baking soda
1 tsp. ground cinnamon
1/4 tsp. ground nutmeg
2 eggs, lightly beaten
1/4 cup molasses
1/4 cup vegetable oil
1 1/2 cups milk
1 1/4 cups grated carrots
1/2 cup chopped toasted walnuts
1/2 cup chopped raisins

Directions:

1. Preheat oven to 400 degrees F (200 degrees C).
2. Grease 36 muffin cups, or use paper liners.
3. In a large bowl, combine flour, bran, wheat germ, brown sugar, baking soda, cinnamon, and nutmeg.
4. Make a well in the center.
5. In a small bowl, mix together eggs, molasses, vegetable oil, milk, and grated carrots.
6. Pour into well, and mix just until moistened.
7. Stir in walnuts and raisins. Fill muffin cups 3/4 full.
8. Bake in preheated oven for 20 to 25 minutes, or until tops spring back when lightly tapped.

Chocolate Chip Carrot Cake Muffins

Ingredients:

2 cups all-purpose flour
2 cups white sugar
1 cup shredded coconut
2 tsps. ground cinnamon
1 tsp. baking soda
1/2 tsp. ground nutmeg
1/2 tsp. salt
2 cups shredded carrots
1 1/2 cups oil
1 (8 oz.) can crushed pineapple
3 eggs
2 tsps. vanilla extract
1 (6 oz.) pkg. chocolate chips

Directions:

1. Preheat oven to 350 degrees F (175 degrees C).
2. Grease 12 muffin cups or line with paper liners.
3. Whisk flour, sugar, coconut, cinnamon, baking soda, nutmeg, and salt together in a large bowl.
4. Add carrots, oil, pineapple, eggs, and vanilla extract and mix until batter is evenly combined.
5. Fold chocolate chips into batter; spoon into the prepared muffin cups.
6. Bake in the preheated oven until a toothpick inserted in the center of a muffin comes out clean, 15 to 30 minutes.
7. Cool muffins for 20 minutes before serving.

Carrot Cake Muffins

Ingredients:

1 cup milk
2 eggs
2 tbsps. applesauce, or more as needed
1 1/2 tsps. vanilla extract
2 cups all-purpose flour
2/3 cup white sugar
1 tbsp. baking powder
1 1/2 tsps. ground cinnamon
1/2 tsp. salt
1 cup shredded carrots
6 tbsps. unsalted butter, melted and cooled

Directions:

1. Preheat oven to 375 degrees F (190 degrees C).
2. Grease 12 muffin cups or line with paper muffin liners.
3. Beat milk, eggs, applesauce, and vanilla extract together in a bowl. Whisk flour, sugar, baking powder, cinnamon, and salt together in another bowl.
4. Stir carrots into flour mixture.
5. Fold in milk mixture and butter until batter is just combined.
6. Spoon batter into prepared muffin cups.
7. Bake in the preheated oven until a toothpick inserted into the center of a muffin comes out clean, 18 to 20 minutes.
8. Cool in the pan for 5 minutes before removing to a wire rack to cool completely.

Carrot Cake Cream Cheese Muffins

Ingredients:

2 1/4 cups all-purpose flour
1/3 cup white sugar
2 tsps. baking soda
1/4 cup margarine, softened
1/2 cup egg substitute
1 cup buttermilk
2 tbsps. frozen orange juice concentrate
1 tbsp. vanilla extract
1 cup grated carrots
1/2 cup raisins, plumped and drained
6 tbsps. cream cheese, softened
2 tbsps. sour cream
1/3 cup white sugar
1/2 cup finely chopped walnuts

Directions:

1. Preheat oven to 350 degrees F (175 degrees C).
2. Grease muffin cups or line with paper liners.
3. In a large bowl, stir together the flour, 1/3 cup of sugar, and baking soda.
4. Add the margarine, buttermilk, egg substitute, orange juice, and vanilla, mix until smooth, then stir in the carrots and raisins.
5. Fill each of the prepared muffin cups 2/3 full.
6. In a small bowl, mix together the cream cheese, sour cream, and remaining 1/3 cup of sugar, until smooth, then stir in the walnuts.
7. Drop a spoonful of the cream cheese mixture onto the top of each cup of muffin batter.
8. Bake at 350 degrees F (175 degrees C) for 20 to 25 minutes, or until golden brown.
9. Remove from the pan and place on a wire rack to cool completely.

Carrot Oatmeal Muffins

Ingredients:

1 cup all-purpose flour
1 cup whole wheat flour
2 tsps. baking soda
1 tsp. baking powder
1/4 tsp. salt
1 tsp. cinnamon
3/4 cup white sugar
3/4 cup brown sugar
1 cup canola oil
3 eggs, beaten
1 tsp. vanilla extract
1/2 cup uncooked rolled oats
1/2 cup flaked coconut
1/2 cup raisins
2 cups shredded carrots
1 (8 oz.) can crushed pineapple, drained with juice reserved
1/4 cup softened cream cheese

Directions:

1. Preheat oven to 350 degrees F (175 degrees C).
2. Lightly grease muffin tins.
3. In a large bowl, mix the all-purpose flour, whole wheat flour, baking soda, baking powder, salt, and cinnamon.
4. Make a well in the center of the mixture, and add white sugar, brown sugar, canola oil, eggs, and vanilla.
5. Mix just until evenly moist.
6. Fold in the oats, coconut, raisins, carrots, and pineapple.
7. In a bowl, blend the reserved pineapple juice and cream cheese.
8. Fill each muffin cup about 1/2 full with the muffin batter, reserving about 1/3 of the batter.
9. Spoon about 1 tsp. of the cream cheese mixture into the muffin cups.
10. Top with remaining batter, so that each muffin cup is about 2/3 full.
11. Bake 25 minutes in the preheated oven, or until a knife inserted in the center of a muffin comes out clean.

Carrot Bran Flax Muffins

Ingredients:

1 1/2 cups all-purpose flour
3/4 cup ground flax seed
3/4 cup oat bran
1 cup brown sugar
2 tsps. baking soda
1 tsp. baking powder
1 tsp. salt
2 tsps. ground cinnamon
3/4 cup skim milk
2 eggs, beaten
1 tsp. vanilla extract
2 tbsps. vegetable oil
2 cups shredded carrots
2 apples, peeled, shredded
1/2 cup raisins
1 cup chopped mixed nuts

Directions:

1. Preheat oven to 350 degrees F (175 degrees C).
2. Grease muffin pan or line with paper muffin liners.
3. In a large bowl, mix together flour, flax seed, oat bran, brown sugar, baking soda, baking powder, salt and cinnamon.
4. Add the milk, eggs, vanilla and oil; mix until just blended.
5. Stir in the carrots, apples, raisins and nuts.
6. Fill prepared muffin cups 2/3 full with batter.
7. Bake at 350 F (175 degrees C) for 15 to 20 minutes, or until a toothpick inserted into the center of a muffin comes out clean.

Carrot Zucchini Multigrain Muffins

Ingredients:

1 1/2 cups all-purpose flour
3/4 cup whole wheat flour
3/4 cup oat flour
1 tsp. salt
1 tsp. baking soda
1 tsp. baking powder
2 1/2 tsps. ground cinnamon
1/4 tsp. ground nutmeg
3 eggs
1/2 cup vegetable oil
1/2 cup unsweetened applesauce
1 cup plain yogurt
1 cup white sugar
3/4 cup honey
2 tsps. vanilla extract
1 cup shredded zucchini
1 cup shredded carrots
1/2 cup chopped pecans
1/2 cup raisins

Directions:

1. Preheat oven to 400 degrees F (200 degrees C).
2. Lightly grease 24 muffin cups.
3. In a bowl, sift together the all-purpose flour, whole wheat flour, oat flour, salt, baking powder, baking soda, cinnamon, and nutmeg.
4. In a separate bowl, beat together eggs, vegetable oil, applesauce, yogurt, sugar, honey, and vanilla.
5. Mix the flour mixture into the egg mixture.
6. Fold in the zucchini, carrots, pecans, and raisins.
7. Scoop into the prepared muffin cups.
8. Bake 18 to 20 minutes in the preheated oven, until a toothpick inserted in the center of a muffin comes out clean.
9. Cool 10 minutes before transferring to wire racks to cool completely.

Apple Carrot Muffins

Ingredients:

1 3/4 cups bran cereal
1 1/4 cups all-purpose flour
3/4 cup white sugar
1 1/4 tsps. baking soda
1 tsp. ground cinnamon
1/4 tsp. salt 1 egg
3/4 cup buttermilk
1/4 cup canola oil
3/4 cup peeled chopped apple
3/4 cup grated carrot
1/4 cup chopped walnuts

Directions:

1. Preheat oven to 400 degrees F (200 degrees C).
2. Line 12 muffin cups with paper liners.
3. Mix bran cereal, flour, sugar, baking soda, cinnamon, and salt together in a bowl. Beat egg, buttermilk, and canola oil in a separate bowl.
4. Pour liquid ingredients into bran mixture; gently stir in apple, carrot, and walnuts.
5. Spoon batter into prepared muffin cups, filling them about 3/4 full.
6. Bake in the preheated oven until a toothpick inserted into the center of a muffin comes out clean, 20 to 25 minutes.
7. Cool in pans for 5 minutes before removing muffins to finish cooling on a wire rack.

Carrot and Cranberry Muffins

Ingredients:

1 cup all-purpose flour
1 cup whole wheat flour
1 tbsp. chia seeds
2 tsps. baking powder
1/2 tsp. salt
1/2 tsp. ground cinnamon
1/4 tsp. ground nutmeg
1/4 tsp. ground ginger
1/2 cup unsalted butter, room temperature
1/2 cup brown sugar, or to taste
1/4 cup white sugar, or to taste
1 egg
1 banana
2 cups grated carrots
1 tbsp. grated orange zest
3/4 cup cranberries, or more to taste

Directions:

1. Preheat oven to 375 degrees F (190 degrees C).
2. Line 12 muffin cups with paper liners.
3. Mix all-purpose flour, whole wheat flour, chia seeds, baking powder, salt, cinnamon, nutmeg, and ginger together in a large bowl.
4. Beat butter, brown sugar, and white sugar together with an electric mixer in a large bowl until light and fluffy.
5. Beat egg into the butter mixture.
6. Mash banana into the butter mixture until smoothly incorporated. Fold carrot and orange zest into the mixture.
7. Mix flour mixture into the butter mixture about 1/2 cup at a time to make a batter.
8. Fold cranberries into the batter. Divide evenly between prepared muffin cups to fill nearly to the top.
9. Bake in the preheated oven until a toothpick inserted into the center comes out clean, 20 to 30 minutes.
10. Cool in the pans for 5 minutes before removing to cool completely on a wire rack.

Carrot Cake with Bourbon Cheesecake Swirl

Carrot Cake Ingredients:

1 1/4 cups all-purpose flour
1 tsp. baking powder
1 tsp. pumpkin spice
1/2 tsp. baking soda
1/2 cup butter, at room temperature
1/2 cup packed brown sugar
2 eggs, lightly beaten
1/4 cup plain yogurt
1 cup packed finely grated carrots
Cream Cheese Filling:
1 (4 oz.) pkg. cream cheese, softened
1/4 cup white sugar
1 egg, lightly beaten
3 tbsps. all-purpose flour
1 tbsp. bourbon whiskey
1 tsp. grated orange zest

Directions:

1. Preheat oven to 350 degrees F (175 degrees C).
2. Line a 9x5-inch loaf pan with parchment paper.
3. Sift 1 1/4 cup flour, baking powder, pumpkin spice, and baking soda together in a bowl.
4. Combine butter and brown sugar in another bowl.
5. Beat together with an electric mixer on low until light and fluffy. Whisk in eggs and yogurt.
6. Beat in carrots until well mixed.
7. Add flour mixture gradually with the electric mixer until combined.
8. Beat cream cheese, white sugar, egg, 3 tbsps. flour, bourbon, and orange zest together in a bowl.
9. Pour half of the batter into the prepared pa.
10. Spread with a spatula until even.
11. Spoon cream cheese mixture onto the batter.
12. Smooth with the back of the spoon until even.
13. Pour remaining batter onto the cream cheese mixture.
14. Bake in the preheated oven until a toothpick inserted into the center comes out clean, 40 to 45 minutes.

15. Cool in the pan for 5 minutes before removing to cool completely on a wire rack.

Carrot Pineapple Cake

Ingredients:

1 cup butter
1 cup white sugar
1 cup packed light brown sugar
3 eggs
2 1/2 cups all-purpose flour
1/2 tsp. salt
2 tsps. ground cinnamon
2 tsps. baking soda
1 tsp. baking powder
2 tsps. vanilla extract
1 cup grated carrots
1 cup crushed pineapple, drained
1 cup chopped walnuts

Directions:

1. Preheat oven to 325 degrees F (165 degrees C).
2. Grease and flour two 8 inch round cake pans.
3. In a medium bowl, cream together the butter, white sugar and brown sugar.
4. Stir in the eggs one at a time beating well after each.
5. Sift together the flour, salt, cinnamon, baking soda and baking powder, stir into the creamed mixture.
6. Finally stir in the vanilla, carrots, pineapple and walnuts. Divide batter evenly between the two pans.
7. Bake for 60 to 75 minutes in the preheated oven.
8. Test for doneness with a toothpick.

Carrot Walnut Cake

Ingredients:

3 cups all-purpose flour
2 tsps. baking powder
1 tsp. baking soda
1 tsp. ground cinnamon
1/2 tsp. salt
1 cup butter, softened
1 cup light brown sugar
1 cup white sugar
4 eggs
1/8 cup orange juice
1 cup chopped walnuts
1 cup raisins
4 cups grated carrots
1 (8 oz.) package cream cheese
1 tsp. vanilla extract
1/2 cup butter
1 1/3 cups confectioners' sugar

Directions:

1. Preheat oven to 350 degrees F (175 degrees C).
2. Grease and flour a 10 inch round cake pan. Sift together the flour, baking powder, baking soda, cinnamon and salt, set aside.
3. In a medium bowl, cream together the 1 cup butter, brown sugar and white sugar.
4. Stir in the eggs and the orange juice.
5. Add the sifted dry ingredient, mix well. Finally, fold in the walnuts, raisins and carrots.
6. Pour the batter into the prepared pan.
7. Bake for 1 hour in the preheated oven, until a tester comes out clean. Cool in the pan for 10 minutes before inverting onto a wire rack.
8. To make the frosting, in a medium bowl, beat together the cream cheese, vanilla, 1/2 cup butter and confectioners sugar until smooth.
9. Spread over cooled cake.

Carrot Cookies

Ingredients:

1 cup shortening
3/4 cup white sugar
2 eggs
1 cup mashed cooked carrots
2 tsps. baking powder
2 cups all-purpose flour
1/2 tsp. salt
3/4 cup shredded coconut

Directions:

1. Preheat oven to 400 degrees F (200 degrees C).
2. Lightly grease cookie sheets.
3. Mix shortening, sugar, eggs, and carrots.
4. Blend in flour, baking powder and salt.
5. Stir in coconut.
6. Drop dough by teaspoonfuls about 2 inches apart onto lightly greased baking sheet.
7. Bake 8 to 10 minutes or until no imprint remains when touched lightly. Immediately remove baking sheet. Let cool.

Peanut Butter Carrot Cookies

Ingredients:

1/2 cup butter
1/2 cup packed brown sugar
3/4 cup white sugar
1/2 cup peanut butter
1 egg
1/4 cup milk
1 cup all-purpose flour
1/4 tsp. salt
1/2 tsp. baking soda
2 cups rolled oats 1 cup grated carrots
1 cup semisweet chocolate chips

Directions:

1. Preheat oven to 375 degrees F (190 degrees C).
2. Cream together the margarine, brown sugar, white sugar, and peanut butter.
3. Add in the egg and the milk. Sift together the flour, salt and baking soda and stir in.
4. Stir in oats.
5. Add in the carrots and chocolate chips. Drop by tsp. onto cookie sheets and bake for 15 minutes.

Carrot-Cranberry Cake

Cake Ingredients:

1 3/4 cups all-purpose flour
2 tsps. baking soda
2 tsps. baking powder
2 tsps. ground cinnamon
1/2 tsp. salt
1/2 tsp. ground allspice
1 1/2 cups granulated sugar
1 cup mayonnaise or sour cream
3 eggs
1 tbsp. ginger-flavored brandy or water
2 cups shredded carrots (about 4 medium)
1 can (8 oz.) crushed pineapple in juice, undrained
1/2 cup chopped pecans or walnuts
1/2 cup sweetened dried cranberries
Cream Cheese Frosting
2 pkgs. (3 oz. each) cream cheese, softened
3 tbsps. butter or margarine, softened
1/2 tsp. ginger-flavored brandy or vanilla
1/8 tsp. salt, if desired
2 1/2 to 3 cups powdered sugar
Sugared cranberries
Sugared orange peel

Directions:

1. Heat oven to 350 degrees F.
2. Grease bottom and sides of three 8-inch square pans or three 8-inch round cake pans with shortening; lightly flour.
3. Mix flour, baking soda, baking powder, cinnamon, 1/2 tsp. salt and the allspice; set aside.
4. In large bowl, beat granulated sugar, mayonnaise and eggs with electric mixer on medium speed, scraping bowl occasionally, until blended.
5. Beat in 1 tbsp. brandy.
6. Gradually beat in flour mixture until batter is smooth.
7. Stir in carrots, pineapple, pecans and dried cranberries.
8. Pour into pans.
9. Bake 30 to 35 minutes or until toothpick inserted in center comes out clean.
10. Cool 10 minutes; remove from pans to wire rack.
11. Cool completely, about 1 hour.

12. In medium bowl, beat cream cheese, butter, 1/2 tsp. brandy and 1/8 tsp. salt on medium speed until smooth.
13. Gradually beat in powdered sugar on low speed until smooth and spreadable.
14. Fill layers and frost side and top of cake with frosting. Garnish with cranberries and orange peel.
15. Store covered in refrigerator.

Carrot Cake Quick Bread

Bread Ingredients:

1 box yellow cake mix
1/2 cup vegetable oil
1/2 cup water
4 eggs
2 tsps. ground cinnamon
1/2 tsp. ground nutmeg
2 cups shredded carrots (3 medium)
1/3 cup chopped walnuts
Frosting
4 oz. cream cheese, softened
2 tbsps. butter, softened
3/4 cup powdered sugar
1/4 tsp. vanilla

Directions:

1. Heat oven to 350 degrees F.
2. Spray bottoms only of two 8x4-inch loaf pans with cooking spray.
3. In large bowl, beat cake mix, oil, water, eggs, cinnamon and nutmeg with electric mixer on medium speed 2 minutes, scraping bowl occasionally.
4. Stir in carrots and walnuts.
5. Divide batter evenly between pans.
6. Bake 40 to 45 minutes or until toothpick inserted in center comes out clean.
7. Cool 10 minutes. Run knife around edges to loosen loaf.
8. Remove from pans to cooling rack. Cool completely, about 1 hour.
9. In small bowl, beat Frosting ingredients with spoon until smooth. Frost tops of loaves.
10. When ready to serve, cut into slices.
11. Cover and refrigerate any remaining bread.

Ginger Carrot Cake

Carrot Cake Ingredients:

1 tbsp. all-purpose flour
1/4 cup finely chopped crystallized ginger
1 1/4 cups all-purpose flour
3/4 cup granulated sugar
3/4 cup vegetable oil
2 tsps. ground cinnamon
1 tsp. baking soda
1/2 tsp. salt
1/4 tsp. ground nutmeg
2 tsps. vanilla
2 eggs
1 1/2 cups shredded carrots

Frosting Ingredients:

1 package (3 oz.) cream cheese, softened
1/4 cup butter or margarine, softened
2 cups powdered sugar
1 tsp. vanilla

Directions:

1. Heat oven to 350 degrees F.
2. Grease bottom and sides of square pan, with shortening.
3. Toss 1 tbsp. flour and the ginger to coat; set aside.
4. In large bowl, beat all remaining carrot cake ingredients with electric mixer on low speed 30 seconds.
5. Beat on medium speed 3 minutes.
6. Stir in carrots and ginger-flour mixture.
7. Pour into pan.
8. Bake 30 to 35 minutes or until toothpick inserted in center of cake comes out clean.
9. Cool completely on wire rack, about 1 hour.
10. Meanwhile, in medium bowl, beat cream cheese and butter on medium speed until smooth.
11. Gradually stir in powdered sugar and 1 tsp. vanilla until smooth and spreadable.
12. Spread cream cheese frosting on cake.

Morning Glory Carrot Cake

Cake Ingredients:

1 box yellow cake mix
3 tbsps. whole wheat flour
1 1/4 cups water
1/2 cup vegetable oil
4 eggs
1 1/2 tsps. ground cinnamon
1/4 tsp. ground nutmeg
2 1/2 cups finely shredded carrots (about 5 medium)
1/3 cup raisins
1/3 cup chopped walnuts

Frosting Ingredients:

3 cups powdered sugar
1 pkg. (8 oz.) cream cheese, softened
2 tbsps. butter or margarine, softened
1 tsp. vanilla
3/4 cup flaked coconut, toasted

Directions:

1. Heat oven to 350 degrees F (or 325 degrees F for dark or nonstick pan).
2. Spray bottom and sides of 13x9-inch pan with baking spray with flour.
3. In large bowl, stir cake mix and flour.
4. Reserve 1/3 cup cake mix mixture.
5. To remaining mixture, add water, oil, eggs, cinnamon and nutmeg; beat with electric mixer on low speed 30 seconds, then on medium speed 2 minutes, scraping bowl occasionally.
6. In medium bowl, stir carrots, raisins, walnuts and reserved cake mix mixture until coated.
7. Stir into batter; pour into pan.
8. Bake 35 to 43 minutes or until toothpick inserted in center comes out clean. Cool completely, about 2 hours.
9. In large bowl, beat powdered sugar, cream cheese, butter and vanilla on low speed until blended.
10. Beat on medium speed until smooth and creamy.
11. Spread frosting over cake.
12. Sprinkle with coconut.

Chocolate Carrot Cake

Cake Ingredients:

1 box chocolate fudge cake mix
Water, vegetable oil and eggs called for on cake mix box
2 tsps. ground cinnamon
3 cups shredded carrots (5 med.)

Directions:

1. Heat oven to 350 degrees F.
2. Spray bottom only of 13x9-inch pan with cooking spray.
3. In large bowl, make cake mix as directed on box.
4. Beat in cinnamon.
5. Stir in carrots.
6. Pour into pan.
7. Bake 30 to 35 minutes or until toothpick inserted in center comes out clean.
8. Cool completely, about 1 hour.
9. In large bowl, beat cream cheese and butter with electric mixer on medium-high speed until smooth.
10. Beat in vanilla. On low speed, beat in powdered sugar until frosting is smooth and creamy.
11. Spread on top of cake.
12. Cut into 4 rows by 3 rows.
13. Cover and refrigerate any remaining cake.

Baked Carrot Cake Doughnuts

Ingredients:

1 1/4 cups all-purpose flour
3/4 cup granulated sugar
1/2 tsp. baking powder
1/4 tsp. salt
1 tsp. ground cinnamon
1/4 tsp. ground nutmeg
1 egg
2/3 cup vegetable oil
1/2 cup milk
1 tbsp. molasses
1 tsp. vanilla
1/2 cup finely grated carrot
1 pkg. (3 oz.) cream cheese, softened
2 tbsps. milk
1 cup powdered sugar
1/4 cup chopped pecans, if desired

Directions:

1. Heat oven to 350 degrees F.
2. Lightly spray 6-cup doughnut pan with cooking spray.
3. In medium bowl, stir together flour, granulated sugar, baking powder, salt, cinnamon and nutmeg with whisk.
4. In 4-cup measuring cup, beat egg, oil, milk, molasses, vanilla and carrot with whisk.
5. Pour wet ingredients into dry ingredients; fold until just combined.
6. Spoon or pipe batter into donut cups, filling about half full.
7. Bake on center oven rack 10 to 12 minutes or until doughnuts are golden around edges and spring back when touched.
8. Remove from oven.
9. Turn doughnuts out onto cooling rack.
10. Repeat with remaining batter.
11. In small bowl, beat cream cheese, milk and powdered sugar with electric mixer on medium speed until smooth.
12. Spread on cooled donuts.
13. Sprinkle pecans over tops.

Carrot Cake Whoopie Pies

Cookies Ingredients:

2 cups all-purpose flour
1 1/2 tsps. baking soda
1 tsp. baking powder
1 tsp. ground cinnamon
1 tsp. ground ginger
1/2 tsp. salt
1/2 tsp. freshly ground nutmeg
1/2 cup butter, softened
1/2 cup granulated sugar
1/2 cup packed light brown sugar
2 eggs
2 tsps. vanilla
1 1/2 cups grated carrots
1/2 cup sweetened flaked coconut
1/2 cup chopped pecans
Maple-Cream Cheese Filling
1 cup butter, softened
1 package (8 oz.) cream cheese, softened
1/4 cup real maple syrup
1 tsp. vanilla
2 cups powdered sugar
Garnish
1/2 cup finely chopped pecans or shredded coconut

Directions:

1. Heat oven to 350 degrees F.
2. Line cookie sheets with parchment paper.
3. In small bowl, stir together flour, baking soda, baking powder, cinnamon, ginger, salt and nutmeg; set aside.
4. In large bowl, beat 1/2 cup butter, the granulated sugar and brown sugar with electric mixer on medium speed about 5 minutes or until light and fluffy.
5. Beat in eggs, one at a time, scraping bowl after each addition. Beat in 2 tsps. vanilla.
6. Add carrots, coconut and pecans; beat on low speed until combined.
7. Using ice cream scoop, drop batter onto cookie sheets at least 2 inches apart to make 30 cookies.
8. Bake 12 minutes or until cookies are set; do not overbake. Cool 5 minutes.

9. Remove from cookie sheets to cooling racks.
10. Cool completely, about 30 minutes.
11. In small bowl, beat 1 cup butter and the cream cheese with electric mixer on medium speed about 5 minutes or until light and fluffy. Beat in syrup and 1 tsp. vanilla.
12. Slowly add powdered sugar, beating until filling is smooth.
13. Sandwich filling between 2 cookies.
14. Roll whoopie pies in pecans or coconut.

Scalloped Carrots

Ingredients:

12 carrots, peeled and sliced
1/4-inch thick
1/3 cup butter
1 onion, minced
3 cloves garlic, minced
1/4 cup all-purpose flour
Salt to taste
2 cups milk
1 1/2 cups cubed Cheddar cheese, or to taste
1/4 tsp. mustard powder
1/4 tsp. white pepper
1/4 tsp. celery seed
1/2 tsp. salt
2 tbsps. butter, melted
1 cup soft bread crumbs

Directions:

1. Preheat oven to 350 degrees F (175 degrees C).
2. Lightly grease a 2-quart casserole.
3. Place carrots into a large pot and cover with salted water.
4. Bring to a boil.
5. Reduce heat to medium-low and simmer until tender, about 4 to 6 minutes.
6. Drain and transfer to a large bowl.
7. Melt 1/3 cup butter in a heavy saucepan over low heat.
8. Cook and stir onion and garlic in the melted butter until tender, 5 to 10 minutes.
9. Season with salt. Whisk flour into onion mixture until smooth; cook, stirring constantly, until flour mixture is a paste-like consistency and light brown, 5 to 10 minutes.
10. Increase heat to medium; gradually stream milk into flour mixture until thick and bubbly, 5 to 10 minutes.
11. Whisk Cheddar cheese, about 2 tbsps. at a time, stirring until cheese melts each time before adding more, forming a smooth sauce, 10 to 15 minutes.
12. Stir in mustard powder, white pepper, celery seed, and 1/2 tsp. salt until incorporated, 1 to 2 minutes.
13. Pour sauce over carrots and toss to coat.
14. Transfer to the prepared casserole dish.

15. Mix 2 tbsps. melted butter and bread crumbs together in a bowl until well coated; sprinkle over carrot mixture.
16. Bake in the preheated oven until sauce is bubbling and topping is browned, 25 to 30 minutes.

Carrots Au Gratin

Ingredients:

4 1/2 cups sliced carrots
2/3 cup crushed buttery round crackers
3 tbsps. margarine, melted
1/2 cup chopped onion
3 tbsps. all-purpose flour
1/2 tsp. salt
1/4 tsp. ground black pepper
1 1/2 cups milk
2/3 cup shredded processed cheese

Directions:

1. Preheat oven to 350 degrees F (175 degrees C).
2. Place carrots in a steamer over 1 inch of boiling water, and cover.
3. Cook until tender but still firm, about 6-10 minutes.
4. Drain.
5. Meanwhile, in a small bowl combine crushed crackers with 1 tbsp. melted margarine.
6. Mix well and set aside.
7. In a medium skillet over low heat, heat the remaining 2 tbsps. of margarine and saute onions until tender.
8. Stir in flour, salt and pepper.
9. Cook for a few minutes, stirring to prevent browning.
10. Gradually pour in milk, stirring constantly. Increase heat to medium and cook until bubbly and thickened.
11. Add cheese and stir until smooth. Fold in carrots.
12. Pour mixture into a 9x12 inch baking dish and sprinkle with the crumb mixture.
13. Bake in preheated oven for 20 minutes, or until bubbly and golden brown.

Cheesy Carrots

Ingredients:

2 lbs. carrots, cut into 2 inch pieces
2 tbsps. butter
1 onion, minced
8 oz. sharp Cheddar cheese, shredded
1 green bell pepper, minced
1/4 cup fresh parsley, chopped
Salt and pepper to taste
3/4 cup dry bread crumbs

Directions:

1. In a large pot of water, boil carrots until soft.
2. Drain well.
3. Preheat oven to 350 degrees F (175 degrees C).
4. Grease a 9x13 inch casserole dish.
5. Place carrots in a large mixing bowl and mash them well.
6. Stir in butter, onion, cheese, green pepper, parsley, salt and pepper.
7. Transfer to the prepared baking dish and top with bread crumbs.
8. Bake in a preheated 350 degrees F (175 degrees C) oven for 40 minutes.

Whipped Carrots and Parsnips

Ingredients:

1 1/2 pounds carrots, coarsely chopped
2 pounds parsnips, peeled and cut into large pieces
1/2 cup butter, diced
1 pinch ground nutmeg
Salt to taste
Ground black pepper to taste

Directions:

1. Bring a large pot of salted water to a boil.
2. Add carrots, cover partially, and simmer 5 minutes.
3. Add parsnips, and cover partially. Simmer until vegetables are very tender, about 15 minutes.
4. Drain well.
5. Return vegetables to saucepan, and stir over medium heat until any excess moisture evaporates.
6. Transfer to food processor.
7. Add butter, and process until smooth.
8. Season with nutmeg, salt, and pepper.
9. Serve and enjoy!

Baked Carrots

Ingredients:

1 (16 oz.) pkg. frozen, chopped carrots
1/2 cup light cream
3 1/2 tbsps. prepared horseradish
1 tbsp. grated onion
1 cup mayonnaise
1 tsp. salt
1/4 tsp. black pepper
1/4 cup melted butter
1/2 cup crushed corn flake cereal

Directions:

1. Preheat oven to 350 degrees F (175 degrees C).
2. Place carrots in a 9x13 inch baking dish.
3. In a medium bowl combine cream, horseradish, onion, mayonnaise, salt and pepper.
4. Pour mixture over carrots.
5. Combine melted butter and corn flakes.
6. Sprinkle over carrots.
7. Bake in preheated oven for 15 to 20 minutes, or until heated through.

Honey Glazed Pea Pods and Carrots

Ingredients:

2 cups sliced carrots
1/2 pound snow peas, trimmed
3 tbsps. butter
1/2 tsp. cornstarch
2 tbsps. honey

Directions:

1. Bring a large saucepan of salted water to a boil.
2. Add carrots and cook until tender crisp, 10 to 12 minutes.
3. Add pea pods and cook until tender crisp; drain and set aside.
4. Melt butter in the same pan and stir in cornstarch.
5. Return carrots and peas to pan and stir in honey.
6. Cook over medium heat, stirring occasionally, until heated through.

Honey Rosemary Carrots

Ingredients:

4 large carrots, peeled and cut diagonally into medium slices
1/4 cup water
2 tbsps. butter
1/4 cup honey
1 sprig fresh rosemary, leaves stripped

Directions:

1. Bring carrots, water, and butter to a boil in a small saucepan.
2. Reduce heat to medium and simmer for 10 minutes.
3. Add honey and rosemary; continue simmering until carrots are tender, about 5 minutes more.

Carrot Fritters

Ingredients:

4 carrots, julienned
1 onion, sliceed
1 bunch green onions, chopped
1 cup all-purpose flour
1 tsp. salt
1/4 tsp. ground black pepper
2 eggs
2 quarts oil for deep frying

Directions:

1. In a medium bowl combine carrots, onion, green onions, flour, salt, pepper and eggs; mix well to coat.
2. Heat oil in deep-fryer to 375 degrees F (190 degrees C).
3. Using tongs, pick up veggies and drop into hot oil.
4. Fry 3 minutes on one side and 2 minutes on the other.

Carrot Pepperoni Caesar Salad

Ingredients:

12 carrots, chopped
20 slices pepperoni, cut into eighths
1/4 cup almonds
5 cups shredded lettuce
1 tsp. grated Parmesan cheese
2 cups lemon juice
4 tsps. vinegar
2 cups croutons
1 1/3 cups Caesar dressing
2 tbsps. plain oatmeal

Directions:

1. Toss the carrots, pepperoni, almonds, and lettuce together in a bowl.
2. Top with the Parmesan.
3. Drizzle the lemon juice and vinegar over the salad.
4. Scatter the croutons over the salad.
5. Spread the Caesar dressing over the top.
6. Sprinkle the oatmeal over the salad to serve.

Spicy Beet and Carrot Salad

Ingredients:

Olive oil cooking spray
1 pound carrots - peeled and cut into 1/2-inch pieces
1 onion, cut into 1/2-inch pieces
1 pound beets - peeled and cut into 1/2-inch pieces
1 tbsp. honey
1/4 tsp. ground dried chipotle pepper
1 tsp. Dijon mustard
1 tbsp. olive oil
1/2 cup brewed black tea
2 tsps. apple cider vinegar
1/8 tsp. sea salt
5 cups arugula
2 1/2 oz. crumbled goat cheese

Directions:

1. Preheat oven to 450 degrees F (230 degrees C).
2. Spray a 9x13-inch roasting pan with cooking spray.
3. Place the carrots and onion on one side of the pan, and the beets on the other side. Spray the vegetables with cooking spray.
4. Cover pan with aluminum foil.
5. Roast the vegetables in the preheated oven for 20 minutes, then uncover pan and roast until browned and tender, about 20 more minutes.
6. Whisk together the honey, ground chipotle pepper, Dijon mustard, olive oil, tea, apple cider vinegar, and salt until the mixture is smooth and the salt has dissolved.
7. Place the roasted carrots, onion, and beets into a large bowl, and pour the dressing over the vegetables.
8. Gently toss vegetables to coat with dressing.
9. To serve, place 1 cup of arugula on each of 5 salad plates, then top with 1 cup of the dressed vegetables and 1/2 oz. of goat cheese.

Apple and Carrot Christmas Pudding

Ingredients:

4 carrots, peeled and grated
2 apples, peeled, cored, and grated
1 cup raisins
1 cup fine bread crumbs
1 1/2 cups all-purpose flour
2 tsps. baking powder
2 tsps. ground cinnamon
1 tsp. baking soda
1 tsp. salt
1 tsp. ground nutmeg
1 tsp. ground allspice
2/3 cup butter
1/2 cup white sugar
4 eggs

Directions:

1. Combine the carrots, apples, raisins, and bread crumbs in a bowl.
2. Sift together the flour, baking powder, cinnamon, baking soda, salt, nutmeg, and allspice in a separate small bowl. Cream together the butter, sugar, and eggs in a separate large bowl; stir in the flour mixture.
3. Add the carrot mixture and mix well. Transfer mixture to a lightly-greased, 2-quart mold.
4. Place a steamer rack in the bottom of a large, deep pot. Set the filled mold on top of the steamer rack.
5. Pour enough water into the bottom of the pot to cover the bottom 2/3 of the mold.
6. Bring to a boil over medium heat.
7. Reduce heat to low; cover. Simmer for 2 hours 45 minutes, adding water occasionally to maintain the water level.
8. Remove from water and allow to cool 10 minutes before turning out of mold onto a plate.

Cajun Rainbow Carrot Fries

4 large rainbow carrots, cut into thick strips
1 tbsp. cornstarch
2 tsps. coconut sugar
1 pinch cayenne pepper
1 pinch paprika
1 pinch garlic powder
1 pinch onion powder
1 pinch ground black pepper
1 pinch dried oregano
1 pinch dried thyme
2 tbsps. olive oil

Directions:

1. Preheat oven to 425 degrees F (220 degrees C).
2. Grease a baking sheet.
3. Place carrots in a large bowl.
4. Add cornstarch and toss, using your hands, until evenly coated.
5. Sprinkle coconut sugar, cayenne pepper, paprika, garlic powder, onion powder, black pepper, oregano, and thyme over carrots.
6. Drizzle olive oil over seasoned carrots and toss to coat.
7. Spread carrots onto the prepared baking sheet.
8. Bake in the preheated oven for 15 minutes; flip and continue baking until lightly browned and crispy, 10 to 15 minutes more.

Rainbow Carrot Pickles

Ingredients:

2 lbs. multi-colored carrots
2 tsps. white sugar
4 tsps. pickling salt, divided
1/2 tsp. whole cloves
1 cup water
1 1/2 cups white wine vinegar
1/2 cup honey

Directions:

1. Scrub carrots thoroughly (do not peel), rinse well, and drain. Using a mandoline or food processor, slice into 1/8-inch-thick rounds, discarding tops.
2. Transfer to a colander set over a bowl.
3. Toss with sugar and 1 tsp. salt.
4. Let stand 1 hour, then rinse under cold water; drain.
5. Toast cloves or coriander seeds in a nonreactive 3-quart pot over medium heat, shaking pan, until fragrant, about 1 minute.
6. Carefully pour in water.
7. Stir in vinegar, honey, and remaining 3 tsps. salt.
8. Bring to a boil; add carrots and cook, stirring, just until brine returns to a simmer, about 8 minutes.
9. Spoon carrots into 2 clean quart jars, using a slotted spoon, and pack them in snugly.
10. Carefully pour or ladle enough brine over veggies to cover completely, leaving about 1/2 inch headspace.
11. Wipe rims with a damp paper towel.
12. Let cool to room temperature, about 1 hour.
13. Apply clean lids.
14. Chill at least 24 hours before eating for best flavor.

Carrot Juice Float

Ingredients:

2 large carrots
1/4 cup vanilla ice cream

Directions:

1. Wash the carrots and trim the tops off, then juice using a juice machine.
2. Pour the carrot juice over the ice cream to serve.

Tempura Carrot Slivers

Ingredients:

1 cup canola oil
1 egg
1 cup ice-cold water
1 cup flour
1/4 tsp. bicarbonate of soda
Sea salt
6 carrots, thinly sliced
Soya sauce, for serving

Directions:

1. Place a saucepan over a high heat and add the canola oil.
2. In a large mixing bowl, whisk together the egg and cold water until light and frothy.
3. Add the flour and bicarbonate of soda and quickly whisk together to form a batter – take care not to overwork the mixture.
4. Season with sea salt.
5. Dip the sliced carrots into the batter and place carefully, in batches, in the hot oil.
6. Fry each batch for 20 seconds or until lightly golden and crisp.
7. Drain on paper towels.
8. Serve with soya sauce.

Carrot Hummus

Ingredients:

1 cup chopped carrots
1 (15 oz.) can garbanzo beans (chickpeas), rinsed and drained
1/4 cup tahini (sesame seed paste)
2 tbsps. lemon juice
2 cloves garlic, quartered
1/2 tsp. ground cumin
1/4 tsp. salt
2 tbsps. snipped fresh parsley
Assorted dippers (pita bread triangles, vegetable sticks, crackers)

Directions:

1. In a covered small saucepan cook carrots in a small amount of boiling water for 6 to 8 minutes or until tender; drain.
2. In a food processor combine cooked carrots, garbanzo beans, tahini, lemon juice, garlic, cumin, and salt.
3. Cover and process until mixture is smooth.
4. Transfer to a small serving bowl.
5. Stir in parsley.
6. Cover with plastic wrap or foil and chill for at least 1 hour or for up to 3 days. If too thick, stir in enough water, 1 tbsp. at a time, until dipping consistency.
7. Serve with assorted dippers.

Turkish Carrot Yogurt Dip

Ingredients:

1/4 cup extra-virgin olive oil
1 3/4 cups carrots, peeled and coarsely shredded (3-4 large)
1/3 cup pine nuts or finely chopped walnuts
3/4 tsp. fine sea salt
1-2 garlic cloves, peeled and crushed into paste
2 cups plain Greek yogurt
Assorted dippers, (flatbread, crackers, raw vegetables)

Directions:

1. Heat the oil in a large skillet over medium-high heat.
2. Add a pinch of the carrots to the oil as a test; if they sizzle, add the remaining carrots and cook, stirring frequently, until they begin to soften, about 6 minutes.
3. Add pine nuts and salt.
4. Reduce heat to medium and continue cooking, stirring occasionally, for 5 or 6 minutes, or until carrots are completely soft and beginning to brown and the pine nuts are golden.
5. Add garlic and cook, stirring, another 30 seconds to 1 minute, or until fragrant.
6. Cool slightly.
7. In a medium bowl, stir the warm carrot mixture into the yogurt.
8. Chill before serving.
9. Drizzle with additional olive oil before serving with assorted dippers.

Peas and Carrot Ribbon Salad

Ingredients:

2 cups shelled fresh peas
1 lb. large carrots
1 cup thinly sliced green onions
1/2 cup honey
1/4 cup white wine vinegar
1/2 tsp. salt
1/4 tsp. ground black pepper

Directions:

1. In a saucepan, cook peas in a small amount of boiling water for 2 to 3 minutes or just until crisp-tender.
2. Drain and rinse with cold running water until cool.
3. Peel carrots. Using a vegetable peeler, peel carrots lengthwise into very thin strips.
4. In a large mixing bowl combine peas, carrots, and green onions.
5. In a small mixing bowl combine honey, vinegar, salt, and black pepper.
6. Pour dressing over vegetables and toss gently.
7. Cover and chill 2 to 4 hours. Serve with a slotted spoon.

Roasted Carrots and Cauliflower with Thyme

Ingredients:

1 lb. carrots, peeled and sliced
1 head cauliflower, trimmed and cut into bite-size florets
3 tbsps. olive oil
2 tbsps. chopped fresh thyme
1 tbsp. minced garlic
1 tsp. salt
1/2 tsp. ground black pepper
1 cup grated Parmesan cheese, or more to taste

Directions:

1. Preheat oven to 400 degrees F (200 degrees C).
2. Combine carrots, cauliflower, olive oil, thyme, garlic, salt, and pepper in a roasting pan; cover with aluminum foil.
3. Bake in the preheated oven for 20 minutes.
4. Remove foil, stir vegetables, and continue cooking until vegetables are tender, about 15 minutes more.
5. Toss vegetables with Parmesan cheese.

Carrot Cake Oatmeal

Ingredients:

4 cups water
1 cup steel-cut oats
1 apple, peeled, cored, and chopped
1/2 cup shredded carrot
1/2 cup raisins
1 tsp. ground cinnamon
1/2 tsp. ground nutmeg
1/2 tsp. ground ginger
1 pinch salt
1 tbsp. butter
3/4 cup chopped pecans
1 tbsp. brown sugar
1/2 cup plain yogurt

Directions:

1. Bring water to a boil in a heavy, large saucepan, and stir in the oats.
2. Reduce heat to a simmer, and cook oats until they begin to thicken, about 10 minutes.
3. Mix in the apple, carrot, raisins, cinnamon, nutmeg, ginger, and salt.
4. Let the oats simmer until tender, about 20 more minutes.
5. While the oats are simmering, melt butter in a skillet over medium-low heat, and stir in the pecans.
6. Toast the nuts until fragrant and lightly browned, 2 to 5 minutes, then sprinkle with brown sugar and stir until sugar has melted and coated the pecans.
7. Serve in bowls, each topped with about 2 tbsps. of the pecan mixture and a dollop of yogurt.

About the Author

Laura Sommers is **The Recipe Lady!**

She is a loving wife and mother who lives on a small farm in Baltimore County, Maryland and has a passion for all things domestic especially when it comes to saving money. She has a profitable eBay business and is a couponing addict. Follow her tips and tricks to learn how to make delicious meals on a budget, save money or to learn the latest life hack!

Visit her Amazon Author Page to see her latest books:

amazon.com/author/laurasommers

Visit the Recipe Lady's blog for even more great recipes:

http://the-recipe-lady.blogspot.com/

Follow the Recipe Lady on **Pinterest**:

http://pinterest.com/therecipelady1

Laura Sommers is also an Extreme Couponer and Penny Hauler! If you would like to find out how to get things for **FREE** with coupons or how to get things for only a **PENNY**, then visit her couponing blog **Penny Items and Freebies**

http://penny-items-and-freebies.blogspot.com/

Other Books by Laura Sommers

- Blackberry Recipes
- Strawberry Recipes
- Blueberry Recipes
- The Peach Cookbook

May all of your meals be a banquet
with good friends and good food.

Printed in Great Britain
by Amazon